FIRST FRIENDS CHURCH LIBRARY
MARION, INDIANA

FORGIVE OUR FORGETTINGS, LORD!

R- Prayer

FORGIVE OUR FORGETTINGS, LORD!

Reflections on Gifts and Promises

Karl E. Lutze

Concordia Publishing House
St. Louis   London

Photo Credits:

UNICEF Photo, page 22
Photograph by Bragg, page 28
Photos by Bob Combs, pages 34, 60, 64, 80
Photograph by Harold M. Lambert, page 50
Photograph by Paul Ockrassa, page 55
Photo by Wallowitch, pages 66, 72, 84, 88, 92

Design by Ed Luhmann

Concordia Publishing House, St. Louis, Missouri
Concordia Publishing House Ltd., London, E. C. 1
Copyright © 1972 Concordia Publishing House
Library of Congress Catalog Card No. 72-81921
ISBN 0-570-03136-2

Manufactured in the United States of America

To my mother and father
and my sisters

CONTENTS

Preface	9
I Didn't Die Last Night	11
I Remember Things and I Forget People	13
My Days Have Been Full of Diversion	16
Arguments, Deceptions, and Pompous Prayers	19
I Need to Remember the Hunger of Others	21
We Cannot Tolerate the Dark	25
A Good Morning for You – for Us	29
Each Day Is Beautiful	31
You Understand These Children	35
The Gift of Knowing Other People	39
I Am So Unimpressively Small	41
Your Hands Stretched Out to Us	43
Night with Its Tiredness	45
In Uncertainty – Your Hand of Strength	47
A Morning That Is New	49
Little Ones – Newborn	53
How Can You Contain Your Anger?	55
Where I've Been, Who I Am, Where I'm Going	59
Through All This – Parents Loved Me	63
In All of These People I Find You	67
Come into This Night	70
Help Me to Rub Sleep from My Eyes	73
Books, Food, People Bore Me	75
Sunday Routine – Old Familiar Pattern	77
Ears, Eyes, Hands, and Lips	81
I Am Part of the Rushing and Changing	85
You Thought of Me Long Ago	89
Break the Quiet with Your Love	93

PREFACE

These prayers are expressions of personal contemplation. Most of them have been used as devotional pieces for various gatherings where people had come together to discuss contemporary issues in the light of the Christian's assignment to be faithful to his Lord. The listeners were invited to "eavesdrop" as the soliloquies were spoken. Now you are invited to listen in and to share these thoughts.

KARL E. LUTZE

I DIDN'T DIE LAST NIGHT

I didn't die last night, Lord.
You intended for me to be alive this day.
      Help me to be alive —
      not merely "look alive,"
      going through motions
      and busying myself
           with what others might see
           and call activity.
Help me to see my life
      as a gift from You,
that I may live it well
      to its fullest,
         recalling the life
         of Jesus Christ,
         Your Son,
             who not only lived His life
             but gave it — for me,
                  to me.
What a profound gift
      and reason for joy!
And what a profound responsibility
      to be entrusted with that life!
And yet I am so entrusted.
The minutes and hours tick off swiftly.
Small matter, though, whether this be my last day
to live that life here, or whether I be given
thousands more! What matters is that I know life —
      that I use my eyes
      to see men rejected and abandoned
      and not walk by on the other side;
      that I hear laughter

in little children's voices
and welcome them with a cup of water
or some other caring gesture,
    and forbid them not
    nor regard them as a nuisance;
that I may go to the side
of those who in their blindness
cannot see beyond themselves —
their own miseries
or their own pleasures —
    to open those eyes
    to the possibilities
    of a full life awaiting them in You;
that I may lovingly minister to ears
that have been deaf to the promises
    of mercy and forgiveness
    and not be silent to them;
that I may be in the back rooms of life
where people who have spoiled their lives
weep and long for Your word of forgiveness
    and a second chance at life,
    and in my presence and friendship
    discover You and Your compassion.
Give me awareness of the life of my Lord —
that life which You have given me,
    that in crowded Bethlehems
    or smelling stables
    or at the side of fishermen or craftsmen
    or in the Breaking of Bread
        with strangers or companions
    You and Your love,
    Your forgiveness,
    Your faithful promises,
    Your strength, and Your joy
May be made known to us.

Amen.

I REMEMBER THINGS AND I FORGET PEOPLE

Good morning, Lord!
It's good indeed.
I rested well. The breakfast was fine.
I'm with my friends.
    Thank You — You're good to me.
There have been many, many mornings
    I could have said that and
    I should have said that,
    but I didn't say that.
I have so much on my mind so many mornings;
Not that I want NOT to thank You.
    But there's so little time to think —
        and if I do not think,
        I find it hard to thank.
    I find myself absorbed
        in making myself presentable,
        tending to the little things
            I should have done last night.
    I have to be in a certain place
        at a certain time
        with certain people.
    And there are other things to remember —
        I remember things
        and I forget people.
I forget people who slept outside last night,
        who had no other place to go —
    people who slept in muddy swamps
        of Vietnam;
    people who slept in alleys
        near beer cans and broken glass;
    people who slept on railroad station

benches till someone asked them
    to move on.
I forget people who went to bed hungry
    and woke up hungry,
        for whom there was no breakfast.
I forget people who could not sleep at all last night —
    people who stayed up all night
        in a New York tenement
        because it was their turn for rat-watch;
    people who hurt so badly
        and could not get relief;
    people who waited outside
        emergency clinics for a loved one;
    people who saw a dear one
        in their home die;
    people who sat up holding a sick
        and crying child;
    those who waited for a loved one
        who never came home
            in one, because he was in an accident;
            in another, because he got drunk;
            in another, because he ran away.
I forget people who have nothing
    to look forward to today —
    another day of fear,
    a day of
        no friends,
        no job,
        no hope.
And now I think
        of the good things I have,
        and even more
        of the good people I have:
            my family and friends.
And I had better think of You who gives all this,
        lest I worship the gifts
        and not the Giver.

O Lord, Giver,
    my Forgiver,
        forgive my forgetting!
        Let my thankfulness be thoughtfulness;
        let my life be a sharing of my life
            with those whose lives are dark and dying.
    Even as Christ . . .
    in whose name I pray.

Amen.

MY DAYS HAVE BEEN FULL OF DIVERSION

Lord Christ,
    who did not let the busyness
        of Your schedule
        divert You
        from seeing little children
        who came to You for a hug;
    who did not first take a survey
        about what others might think
        before You went to the side
        of the woman of shame;
    who did not fall for the appeal
        of well-fed people
        to become their bread-making king;
    who called Peter's plea
        to run from the cross
        devilish;
Lord Christ,
You who still turn not away
from those who call to You
    for forgiveness,
    for help, direction, strength,
    and perseverance,
help me to see that You will not turn away
    from me
        as I call,
    for this day again
    is going to be a day
    of diversions for me.
    My days have been full of diversions
    that have kept me from serving You well,
    from being truly what You intend me to be.

The statistics of other men's crimes
　　　turn me from personal inventory
　　　of my own sins.
The preoccupation with my little
　　　practices of piety
distract me, and I do not see the opportunities
for doing greater and more urgent deeds:
My busyness in rushing to church,
unmindful of the many I pass by —
　　　the hitchhiker,
　　　the driver and his stalled car,
　　　those standing at the side
　　　　　whom I do not know,
　　　whom I cannot even see;
　　　the fellow who awakens
　　　　　from his binge
　　　　　or from his fix
　　　　　to find again
　　　　　the world that has no need,
　　　　　　　no time,
　　　　　　　no place for him;
　　　the woman who fled reality
　　　　　into the bright lights last night
　　　　　and finds it this morning
　　　　　in her empty room;
　　　the children whose parents
　　　　　don't care where they are
　　　　　or if they're clothed
　　　　　and fed;
　　　or people who today
　　　　　have rolled out on highways,
　　　　　hoping to get away
　　　　　and to find themselves
　　　　　and meaning for their lives.
Forgive my forgetting, Lord.
And forgive my remembering You
　　　only as the Man of 2,000 years ago.

I so often have forgotten
    that through Your Word You are here today
    in me
    and in Your other brothers and sisters.
Keep me from a preoccupation with the past
    and from an idle musing on a future after death.
        This day is here — at hand —
        with all its opportunities
        to share the love You've given with those close by
            and those for whom I ought to look around,
                as You once did
                and as You still would do through me —
                Your eyes, Your ears, Your feet,
                Your hands, Your lips that speak Your words
                      of welcome and of love.

Amen.

ARGUMENTS, DECEPTIONS, AND POMPOUS PRAYERS

Deliver me, Lord,
> from lying lips and a deceitful heart.

Deliver me from words persuading me
> that the needs of the needy
>> have been exaggerated.

Deliver me from arguments
> that would discourage me from acts
>> of love,
> that insist that the plight of the poor
>> is their own fault,
> that maintain that government and social agencies
>> have the only responsibility for charity.

Deliver me from rationalizations
> that would justify my walking by on the other side —
> words like
>> "They lie, they cheat, they waste,
>>> they take advantage,
>> they don't appreciate what I do...."

O Lord, make me perceptive
> to the disguise of an evil heart.

Deliver me from its deceptions —
> judging the cries of the poor
> and resenting them
>> because they seem so brazen,
> disdaining the cause of the oppressed
>> because it is presented
>> in words that are crude
>> and uncouth.

Lord, deliver me
> from lying lips and a deceitful heart —
> those of others,
> but even more my own!

Lord, You hear my pompous prayers
    as if I said,
        "I thank You that I'm not like other men":
        this racist,
        that red-neck;
        this phony,
        that hawk;
        this institutional churchman,
        that mayor of Chicago;
        those law-and-order reactionaries,
        that military-industrial complex,
        those fuzz.
You hear my lips speak the human relations jargon:
        voluntary association,
        community,
        Black Power,
        self-determination,
        brotherhood,
        reconciliation.
And my deceiving heart says,
    "Lord, they never have appreciated us,
        have they?"
Let these lips come to Your altar;
        and cleanse them,
        not with coals this time
            but with Bread and Wine,
        remembering the wounded hand
            You raised on Easter
            when You said to my brothers: "Peace!"

Amen.

I NEED TO REMEMBER THE HUNGER OF OTHERS

For the food, Lord, thank You!
But to be really frank with You,
I've grown tired
    of certain kinds of food, Lord;
        and often what's before us to eat
        looks very much
        like what I've had before —
            often.
There are times when I've had dinners
    that I call
        the best meal I've ever eaten;
        and that's a cause for gratitude,
    and I call it
        a regular thanksgiving.
Sometimes when I've missed a meal or two
    (and I admit: That seldom happens!)
        or when I've worked long and hard,
    I've gotten so hungry I didn't care what I ate:
Anything would taste good.
I need to think of such experiences
    so I can begin to be aware
        of what it is to be hungry,
    and can be reminded of hungry people —
        the people I often forget.
I need to be mindful
    of children with empty eyes
        and protruding stomachs;
    of mothers with bony arms
        holding hungry babies
        to their sagging, empty breasts;
    of old men standing in line

        at "gospel-kitchens,"
        willing to be converted for a bowl of soup;
    of little groups in foreign lands
        waiting for a mission truck
        to come with cups of rice
        or milk, hoping there'll be enough
        to go around.
I need to remember
    the children of the crowded cities
        that beg at theater doors
        for old, cold popcorn;
    or men who dig
        through garbage cans of restaurants
        to find the scraps men left behind
        on their plates.
I need to remember
    children crying in the night,
        waking to hunger;
I need to remember
    mothers who weep because,
        going without food themselves,
        they still do not have enough
        for their hungry children;
    fathers who chafe in shame
        and frustration
        because they cannot provide
        what their families need.
My need for remembering these
    is not merely to chastise myself,
        to grovel in my guilt,
    as if feeling bad can somewhat pay
        for my sins of
            forgetfulness,
            ingratitude,
            thoughtlessness,
            selfishness,
            and neglect.

My need for remembering
lies in my need
to see Your goodness,
and my need for Your call to serve,
that I may open my eyes
and ears
and heart
and self
to see those
who wait on You.
The eyes of all wait upon You,
O Lord;
You have opened Your hand
with enough to satisfy
the desire and hunger
of every living thing
in due season.
We have reached out and received.
But our garbage, our throwaway, and waste
speak clearly
and tell us how we have forgotten
those who still reach out in need —
for whom it is past due season.
Lord, forgive;
awaken;
help us to love, to share, and to work;
to meet the hunger of others,
not in words and speech
but in deeds and in truth.

Amen.

WE CANNOT TOLERATE THE DARK

We cannot cope
>with darkness very well, Lord.
>In darkness we bump our shins
>>and stub our toes.
>Cautiously and fearfully
>>we reach out with our hands,
>>our arms stretched and moving
>>>in every direction
>>to touch a branch or corner
>>or extending board
>>that might inflict a pain upon us.
>Scraping our feet we
>>grope our way, sensitive to
>>and wary of
>>>the possibility of obstacle
>>>>or downward stair
>>>>or hole.
>With nostrils raised, intent
>>on detecting the smell of
>>something strange or
>>something familiar —
>with ears alert for any sound,
>we wish we could see what darkness
>>hides from us.
>When men discovered fire
>>and made the night red and bright,
>>they could see,
>>they could keep watch;
>>>and in this they felt safe.
>Now we bathe our cities each night in light
>making dark streets bright as day.

In every room of our homes at least one switch
on the wall can erase the darkness and replace it
with light. Flashlights, floodlights, headlights —
    all say that we cannot stand the dark.
For long years men have set aside
the day for labor
    and the night for sleep,
and the darkness passes faster.
Yet even so, the happenings of the night,
    the fears, the pains, the tragedies all seem worse,
    just because others are sleeping
    — others who might be on hand
    to comfort and to help.
Tonight again, Lord,
darkness comes upon us.
And we seek our lights:
    a fire,
    a candle,
    a lamp;
and we feel a little secure —
    except for the edge
    of the reflection
    where the dark begins.
What is in the shadows?
What is in the night
    we cannot know for sure.
But who is in the shadows
    Who is in the night
    we know.
It is You, who has said: "Fear not,
    I am with you";
It is You, with whom there is no night,
    for darkness and light
        are both alike to You;
It is You, who neither slumbers nor sleeps;
It is You, who hung in darkness,
    black as night,

>>on an early Friday afternoon
that we might never be separated
from God
by our sinfulness.
>It is You, to whom
>>we can pray tonight:
"Lighten our darkness
and guide us in the shadows
and watch us
lovingly as we sleep.

Amen."

A GOOD MORNING FOR ME — FOR US

If I don't view this morning as
         Your morning, as
         Your day,
    made for Your purposes,
    it will not really be as
        good as it could be.
You never did purpose or intend
for people not to have Your love —
    Your love that has made this creation
        and its goodnesses
        for us:
            the sweet juice of a berry,
            the fresh breath of air,
            the cold, refreshing drink of water,
            the smile of friends,
            the affectionate care given
                by a loved one.
These are Your gifts
    intended for men.
And yet some today do not get to
participate in gathering in the gifts
You have intended for all.
Your intended good
    gets roadblocked —
        diverted from its destination —
    by the selfishness of some,
    by the inaction of others;
and for those who do not get the
good You intend for them it is
not a good morning.
Lord,

who made it a good morning
               for me,
give me a renewed
    devotion to not only say:
        "Your will be done"
        but to help implement
        what You intend,
so that Your goodness may not only
be for me
but that through me comes to others,
that people for whom
        so many mornings are not good
            may know
            Your love,
            Your power,
            Your joy,
            Your love;
        through Jesus Christ,
        the Bringer of love and life.

Amen.

EACH DAY IS BEAUTIFUL

Help me discover, O Lord Creator,
in this new day a glimpse
of earth's first day —
    whether full with warm sunshine
        or bathed clean in fresh rain
        or glazed with ice
        or frosted with soft snow
        or even gently wrapped in soft low clouds.
Each day is beautiful and altogether Yours.
How we have spoiled Your days
        with broken bottles, and dented cans,
        and battered hulks of autos,
        and rusted machines — with litter,
        garbage, our fumes, and our waste!
There on the cluttered streets, in the open skies,
        in our once-clear waters, on the road side, in vacant lots,
        and on green hillsides
        lie our spoilings,
        the trophies of our pride and greed.
        But more than laying waste
        the beauties of creation's morn,
we have profaned and trampled human life;
        generation after generation
        has seen the gore of nations
        giving up their youngest best
        to die in pools of blood
        because the older — so-called wiser — men
        could not resolve their disagreements
        without killing.
We have rewarded with praise
        and lavished with respect

>   those who have gained vast hoards
>   of this world's treasures
>   at the cost of the efforts
>   — and even the lives —
>   of others so often
>   deemed unimportant and expendable.

We have developed governments
> that protect
the rich from the poor,
> but that have
notoriously neglected the cause
> of the
less advantaged and have almost encouraged
> their exploitation.
>> The lungs of our children —
>> their minds,
>> their spirit,
>> their optimism —

have been impaired less by malice
than by thoughtlessness, carelessness,
and "actlessness" — by apathy and silence.
> Open my eyes, O Lord, that I may become indignant
>> at that which defaces and destroys
> Your creation and Your creatures.

But more:
> put me in tune with
> Your plans and purposes,
> that I may treasure
> Your forgiveness
> for my own slovenly and wasteful ways
> and respond to Your gifts of life
> by affirming, sustaining, and enriching life
> wherever I find it,
> especially for the good of people:
>> old, young, bright,
>> poor, familiar, distant,
>> strange, prosperous, troubled —

every kind of people,
for You would have me
love them as brothers.
  I pray, thinking of my Brother,
  Jesus Christ.

Amen.

YOU UNDERSTAND THESE CHILDREN

Lord, I was with children today.
How very special is the time of childhood
   with its countless happenings:
      games in the house,
      games on the sidewalks —
         in the snow or ice
         and shivering cold,
      playing with puddles
         or pans and bottles with water,
      or favorite toys,
      or special friends.
I remember calls to come
         to eat,
         or to go to bed,
         or do school work
         or chores
         around the house.
And I remember
   times I was afraid,
   and times I cried when I felt
      pain
      or disappointment —
   and times I laughed so hard
      I could
      hardly stand it any longer!
I remember older people:
   some who had no time for me
      at all,
   some who frightened me,
   some who were an absolute delight
      to be near —

        who could have asked me to do anything,
                and I'd have done it.
I remember when we had "company."
    I remember parades
            and songs;
    I remember shopping
            and getting new clothes;
    I remember pills and medicine
            and getting shots.
I remember school —
    its pencil sharpeners
    and bells;
    a principal and teachers
            and custodian
    and recess
    and report cards
    and vacation.
And I remember church — and getting dressed up
    and sitting still so long,
    and the music.
And I remember hot nights
            and flowers
            and trees for climbing
            and mosquito bites.
But most I remember home:
    the door,
    the table,
    the chairs,
    and the bed — warm and soft
                and comfortable —
    and prayers and efforts at postponing sleep;
    and I remember good food
    and fun
    and love.
For my childhood and Your presence in it, Lord,
protecting, forgiving, causing me to think,
to grow, to have others to love me

and whom I could love —
        I give You thanks.
But then I call to mind tonight
    the many little ones around the world,
    children deprived of childhood:
Some who get to know the streets
        at tender age,
        foraging as best they can
        or begging for a sandwich or a coin;
young ones who've never worn "new clothes,"
whose parents are unable to care for them;
young ones deprived of childhood
because they must become breadwinners
and little fathers or mothers
to their sisters and brothers;
who become old without having known
what it is to be young —
    for whom survival
    becomes a way of life
    and a qualifier of lying
    and greed and of retaliation . . .
    for whom play and good foods
    and fresh air and respect
    and adequate care and full love
    and learning opportunities are not,
        whose future seems a mockery,
        a struggle with
        no hope.
My mind scans the villages of Africa,
the Appalachian hills, the marketplaces of India,
the shanties of the Mississippi countryside,
the crowded streets of Harlem, the settlement
of Indians on a Southwest reservation, the tenements
of Chicago's south side.
    And I can sense
    the restlessness and fear,
    the hopelessness and hurt,

> the frustration and despair,
> the bitterness and anger
> in the people there.
> How long, O Lord?
> > How long their anguish?
> > How long their patience?
> > How long our apathy?
> > How long our silence and inaction?
> How long, O Lord,
> > will You tolerate the prayers
> > of fattened people who pray:
> > > "Give us this day our daily bread"?
> How long, O Lord,
> > will You gently prod and simply say:
> > "When you do no good to these, it is from Me
> > you turn away"?
> How long before You speak
> > Your word of terrible judgment
> > on a world that doesn't care?
> You came once, not to judge or to condemn —
> > You came as a Child.
> And You tasted bitterness,
> rejection, persecution . . .
> You understand
> what these children of poverty endure.
> If You, Lord, should keep score of our sins,
> O Lord, who would survive?
> But with You there is mercy. . . .
> > Forgive me, Lord Christ,
> > and help me to refuse Your children no longer.
> > Make me alert, loving, and eager
> > to find You in children
> > and to serve You well —
> > > as a brother of Yours
> > > > who loves all the Father's children!
>
> Amen.

THE GIFT OF KNOWING OTHER PEOPLE

It's good to meet new people, to make
		new friends, Lord —
		new acquaintances —
to be with
	anyone who helps me
	grow in understanding and insight,
	who helps me know myself better —
	not only my fears,
			my insecurity,
			my smallness,
			and my selfishness —
	but also some of the strengths
		You've given me:
	strength to listen and to learn;
	strength to be impatient with evil and injustice
		but patient with people;
	strength to forgive,
		to trust,
		to risk working together.
	For the gift of knowing myself better
		I am grateful, Lord.
But a gift I dare not overlook
is the gift of knowing other people better:
		people willing to be honest with me,
		people who refuse to be phony,
		people who will not compromise their principles,
		people who cannot forfeit their integrity,
		people who force me to face issues
			from which I've turned away,
		people who in their forthrightness
			do me a service I can never repay.

Lord, I thank You for such people
    and for what You do to me through them,
    their words, their
    actions.
Help me to respond to them in gratitude, in genuineness,
    in love, and keep them strong and persevering.
But lest I forget, O Lord:
    Help me to keep in mind my closest ones
      – the loved ones who are not at my side tonight –
    those who mean so much to me,
    those who selflessly have loved me
    and enriched my life,
those who are older,
those who are my age –
the little ones.
    Give me a grateful and
    joyful heart, remembering them;
and keep them in
    Your gentle,
    watchful care.
Forgive us all, keep us all
    in Your love,
    for the sake of
      Jesus, our Savior
      and
      Brother
      and
      Lord.

Amen.

I AM SO UNIMPRESSIVELY SMALL

Lord,
>of course the big institutions get things done.
>Ford, American, General Motors, and Chrysler
>can spill a million cars out on the highways.
>And chain stores can fill a billion shopping bags
>to stock a billion shelves.
>And public utilities can make cities noon-bright
>at midnight,
>make houses toast-warm in midwinter,
>and splash out refreshing water
>in the driest, hottest summer.
>And government can move countless troops
>while sending two men to the moon,
>and can at the same time scan the skies
>with radar screening.
>And I — I am so unimpressively small
>and unimportant
>and ineffectual.
>If I try to speak out
>and to act on behalf of justice and truth,
>nobody seems to notice.
>If I try to protest against wrongs and injustice,
>nobody even hears.
>And most of the time I don't even try,
>because it all seems so futile.
>And thousands join me in my refrain —
>my refraining to speak.
>And our silence becomes overwhelmingly unanimous.

Lord, lift my sights.
>Help me to see that You expect me
>and enable me to speak —

      to speak as an oracle,
      a spokesman of God;
      to speak as an advocate and champion
      for the poor and neglected,
      the needy and powerless.
Help me to see that You see me,
      and You have noticed my halting,
          my stammering, and my silence.
Help me to see the grief I cause and compound
when I do not convey Your word of concern
for the oppressed.
And forgive my fearfulness and faithlessness.
Open my eyes and ears,
that I may be aware of the plight of the abused.
Let my heart be bursting with Your holy indignation
at the sight of injustice.
And let my lips be opened
and my tongue made free
      to speak the words that expose sin
          but offer hope.
And help me find others
to join in the chorus that once sounded
from the lips of messengers near Bethlehem,
      singing with our voices too
      about Your kind of peace on earth —
      because there is a Savior of all people.
And let our lives be united in concert —
in harmony — with such words.

Amen.

YOUR HANDS STRETCHED OUT TO US

These hands that grip steering wheels
        and flick light switches
        turn door knobs,
        press typewriter keys,
        push brooms,
        lift dish towels and fold laundry,
        guide pencils,
        hold children,
        wield heavy tools,
        count, sort, gesture, wave, or
        manipulate fine instruments
        and intricate machines:
These hands I fold — a symbol of restraint
        of my own activities
        so that I might concentrate on what I am saying
        when I pray, "Into Your hands I commend myself."
Your hands, once tiny,
        holding Your mother's little finger
        or fumbling with a toy;
those hands that rested on the shoulders
        of burdened people,
        that passed out food to throngs,
        that lifted little children high,
        that touched the eyes
        of blind men and made them see again;
those hands that touched fevered brows
        with cooling relief and healing;
        that drew saddened people near;
        that touched corpses, restoring life.
Those hands when raised stilled storms.
Those hands broke bread and passed the cup.

Those hands You surrendered to hammer and nails and death.
Those hands revealing scars were raised to communicate
    to men God's peace, forgiveness, and love.
Those hands stretched out to us beckon and invite —
    and so we come to hands far stronger than our own,
    at Your Hands to receive strength
        for our own weary, failing hands —
    strength to draw away
        from greedy grasping and selfish seizing.
Take these folded hands.
    Open them to receive Your love
    and to share that love with others
        whose hands have long been cold
        and empty
        and far too often crushed
        and crippled
        by selfish and thoughtless people.
You have made us members of Your body,
    forgiving our stiff and unbending paralysis.
Strengthen us to be the hands that reach out in Your name
    to the lonely, the frustrated, the frightened,
    the exhausted, the bitter, and the hopeless
        with Your love,
so that hands everywhere may be raised
    in praise to You,
whose hand is ever upon us to hold us fast and
        to give us peace.

Amen.

NIGHT WITH ITS TIREDNESS

This is the kind of night it was,
   Lord,
when You gathered Your Twelve
      for the supper —
   to many people in many places
   just another night:
      a night that followed
         a day that was
            long
            or
            exciting
            or
            tedious
            or
            painful
            or
            tiring,
but night
with its tiredness
   and darkness.
But for the Twelve it was
a strange and awesome night,
      when You washed their feet
      and You spoke of betrayal
      and You broke bread
      and poured wine,
      and You offered forgiveness
      and strength as You passed the cup.
Strange night as You agonized
      about what You must do
      to grasp our wretchedness from us —

        as You uttered groaning
        prayers for those You
            love.
Could this be such a night,
O Lord,
    a night in which You
    care so deeply
    for us who claim
        to be disciples?
Is this a night for contemplating
our own feet
        — how they have strayed
        in grime and waste
        from paths which You had made;
        — how much they need
        cleansing?
Is this a night to recall
our broken promises
and betrayals?
Is this a night when we might look,
not at our neighbors' sins
but at ourselves and humbly say:
"Lord, is it I?"
Is this a night to look deep into the cup
where love is poured and, beyond
the bread and wine, see
        You,
        Your love,
        Your power, and
        Your life?
Oh, let my lips speak
words from my deepest heart,
words that are Your very own:
        "Your will be done
            with me
            and by me!"

Amen.

IN UNCERTAINTY — YOUR HAND OF STRENGTH

I am not alone tonight —
I never am.
Your hand is ever upon me;
You lead me and hold me fast.
    But I forget, Father!
You have been reliably strong
as I have confronted dangers
in my life while traveling,
        while waiting out storms,
        while going to strange places
        where there were strange people.
When sickness or disaster struck close,
You have sustained me.
It is You who have seen
me choose my own ways
    in mischief, in pride,
    in stubbornness,
    in jealousy, in selfishness.
And yet You have not turned away
from me in anger or disgust.
In this present hour of my
uncertainty and confusion
You point me to my Lord, the Christ,
that I might see the deliberate
and determined steadfastness
with which He set Himself
to the ordeal of crucifixion.
Help me to find in such
rememberings
    His courage,
    His resoluteness,

      His vision,
      His peace,
      His strength and His joy.
These are the gifts You
have for me.
It is You, Father,
who brought me to this hour
and to Your presence;
      forgive my little faith,
      forgive my willingness to promise
      but my slowness to perform,
      forgive my forgettings,
      forgive my past disappointing record.
And comfort me.
Be a fortress to me.
Lay Your hand of strength upon me
      to lead me,
      to hold me fast.

Amen.

A MORNING THAT IS NEW

It is a good morning, Lord!
    Fog, snow, rain, ice, stifling heat,
    or any other variety of inclement
    weather could not change that, Lord.
    And war, and impossibly hard work,
    and severe pain, and having to put up
    with the actions of difficult people,
    and tragic accidents don't keep this
    from being
a good morning, Lord!
    I cannot deny my forgettings,
    my failures, my frustrations,
    my sins, my spoiling of so many
    of Your gifts. I agonize
    to remember them.
And yet the morning is good,
    because it is Your morning,
    Lord. You are in it, and
        You give this morning to us;
a morning that is new;
a morning that — because of
        Easter morning —
    puts aside and forgives
    the yesterdays I've wasted and abused;
    a morning that offers me another chance
        to live well with You —
        live well for You!
It's a good morning,
for You are here with love.
    I see that love as I recall
        the great events of Bethlehem and Golgotha.

      I remember the bread
         and recall drinking from the cup,
         receiving You, my Lord, and Your life.
And Your love comes to me
    through good and kind ones You have placed
    about me here.
Your presence and
the presence of Your love
make it a good morning, Lord.
For some this morning is not all
that it might be — or should be.
    Many have not slept last night
        laboring long hours,
        waiting in fear
           or pain
           or loneliness
           or cold
           or hunger
           for the daylight hours,
           or seeking to forget and drown
           their griefs,
           their disappointments, and
           their hopelessness
           in excursions from reality
           into useless and harmful excesses
           and selfish pleasures.
    Many of these resent
        and would rather sleep through
           this morning,
           for they hate this morning,
           for they do not find You in it
           and they see it only as another beginning
           of another monotonous, hopeless, troubled day
           in which yesterday's unattended needs
           still plague and all but overwhelm them.
Lord, help us, who have seen the goodness
of this morning, to seek out those

for whom mornings are miserable and frightening,
    that we may help remove
    from around them the barriers
    that shield their eyes
    from seeing You,
    that through us Your love
    may come to them —
        attending to their needs,
        affording them understanding,
        according them friendship,
        forgiving and welcoming them,
        enriching their lives,
    that they may see and know You
        and that their mornings
            may be truly good.

Amen.

LITTLE ONES — NEWBORN

This is the first morning for some little children
        lying one next to the other,
some fussing, some howling loudly,
        some sleeping soundly.
All are in antiseptic surroundings,
waiting for the efficient women dressed in white
who do their scheduled chores by chart
        and clock and system.
And there are some who have their first morning
today in little shacks on the back streets of little towns
or in the little shacks on backwoods
        mountain roads,
cared for and loved
but not always well cared
        for and wisely loved.
In other lands today some little ones
        see their first day,
             clasped
             to shriveled breasts of mothers
who themselves have hungered days on end;
and their seems so little chance
        that there will be enough to sustain
        either parent or infant.
To some of the little ones newborn
        this day is a gate to a future of promise —
        promise great,
        promise beautiful.
To some little ones newborn,
        the door of opportunity is
        surely and cruelly shut,
and I had forgotten these this morning.

O Lord, forgive —
and let this remembering be
        more than a pious beating of my breast.
O Lord, let me not rest easy
until I think about these little ones —
and make these thoughts revolve around my mind
and penetrate my heart,
so that I might find some way to
love these little ones
        in more than in mere words or speech,
        but in deed and in truth.
Help me not only to bring
young children unto You
that You should bless them;
Help me to find new ways
to convey Your blessings
to little ones of every
condition:
the blessings
        of love,
        of joy,
        of acceptance,
        of a full
              and fully developed life.
Loving Father,
        who brought me
              through so many mornings,
help me, Your much-loved child,
to share Your spirit of concern
with those in need.
Through Jesus Christ,
        our Lord.

Amen.

HOW CAN YOU CONTAIN YOUR ANGER?

Great God Almighty,
how do you keep Your patience?
    How do You refrain
    from stamping out
    a people that has
        cluttered Your landscapes,
        poisoned Your rivers,
        wasted Your fields,
        and filled the air with filth?

How can You stand
the songs of pride
and the boastful claims
    of those who call themselves
    the most progressive men
    of any age,
    who persist in
    allowing — and supporting —
    a style of life
    that permits disdaining
    and rejecting of fellowmen,
so that hostility bristles
    between blacks and whites,
    Jews and non-Jews,
    labor and management,
    Catholic and Protestants,
    Republicans and Democrats,
    steel hats and students,
    the old and the young?
How can You tolerate
those who in state and in church
    speak words of commitment
    to justice
    and love
    and integrity
    and freedom
    and human rights
but in actions belie their words
and betray those who trust them
and mock the Lord whom they claim
    to serve?
How can You contain Your anger
in the face of those
    who magnify their own resolutions
        and noble performance
    while pointing at others
        who don't measure up,

                    and gloating while racists
                        and bigots are exposed?
            For the profound mystery
                    of a love that forgives,
                    that makes sick creatures well
                    and bestows power
                            on those who have failed
                            and equips them
                            with power and desire to love
            I give you thanks,
                    O Lord!
Take the pride and
        the indifference and
        the selfishness and
        the forgetfulness and
        the inhumanness and
        the coldness
                    that characterize
                    so much of what
                    I think
                    and do
                    and am.
And for the sake of
                    Jesus Christ
                    forgive —
                    and, Lord,
            replace all these foul
            and diseased parts
            of my life
            with the full outpouring
            of the Spirit,
                    so that integrity
                        and courage
                        and wisdom
                        and power
                        and love
                        and faith

                    and joy
            may be the marks of my life.
And let me embrace You
and show to You my love.
            But, Lord —
            You are not here
            to grasp in love,
            to visit with,
            to entertain,
            to keep just for myself.
As I clothe the cold
            and dine the famished
            and serve the thirsty
            and sit with the lonely
            and free the imprisoned
            and comfort the frightened
            and give direction to the confused
            and dignity to the disdained
            and a second chance to the failure
            and welcome to the rejected
            and my love to the despairing —
As I do this
            I give to You
            and love You well.
Empower me for this,
O Lord of love,
                        for Jesus sake.

Amen.

WHERE I'VE BEEN,
WHO I AM, WHERE I'M GOING

Lord, how good it is to draw apart
    from the crowds,
    from books
        and newspapers
        and magazines,
    from highways
        and supermarkets
        and congested traffic
    from sirens
        and giant, noisy trucks,
    from the grinding nature
        of my daily work
    and the thousand
    and more distractions
    that pull at every side,
    from nagging chores
    and unfulfilled commitments.
Lord, how good it is to turn aside
and look at myself —
    where I've been,
    who I am,
    what I'm doing,
    where I'm going,
    why — and take
an inventory of myself;
to count the gifts You've given me:
    forgiveness first of all, and
    grace to call You loving Father,
and other gifts:
    the air I breathe,
    the food I eat,

the water that I drink
 and bathe in,
 that causes seeds to sprout
 and plants to grow,

the shelter that wards off the snow
and sun, and hail and driving rains,
the warmth of a bed and blankets,
the fragrance of flowers,
the lilt of song,
the beauty of sunsets,
and the good health to enjoy it
all;
the people too:
    the young and the old
    who have loved me so warmly,
    who have wept at my pain
    and felt deeply my griefs,
    and were hurt at the times
        that I met disappointment
        and felt my anxieties with me;
    the people who've chided
        and teased me
        and firmly corrected
        and fondly encouraged;
    the people who often delighted
        and surprised me,
    who laughed when I laughed
        and joined when I paused
        to speak prayers of thanksgiving
        for good things You've put into my life.
My cup runs over with
the number and greatness of gifts.
    And now I must stop to remember
    the many about me whose cup is near empty —
        whose rooms are dingy,
        whose health is poor,
        whose nerves are frazzled,
        who tremble with chills
            in the cold of night;
        from whom beauty of life
            seems very well hidden,

for whom God's rich and free gifts
seem so unreal and distant.
Help me in my withdrawing — that I do
not drop from my list of remembering
those who are lonely
and frightened
and running away;
those who feel guilty
and useless
and very unwanted;
those who are hopeless —
who have known no successes,
whose every problem
gives birth to more
and greater ones,
who don't really believe
that prayer works,
that men love,
or that God is.
Help me see them in distant lands,
in dirty ghettos,
or even in our cities' offices
and in our schools.
Make me remember these too,
that as I withdraw
for perspective
and strength,
new insights
and vision
I may with Your joy
seek ways to bring that love
with which I have been so well loved
to the unloved;
in the name of Him who said "Come!"
and says also "Go!"

Amen.

THROUGH ALL THIS — PARENTS WHO LOVED ME

I want to remember my parents, Lord.
I want to reflect on my childhood:
    days of play and mischief
    and laughing
    and running and shouting
    and eating and gulping down
    huge glasses
    of refreshment;
    days that ended in near exhaustion;
    days that saw me resenting
    their end and protesting
    my being sent to bed;
    days after which came
    nights of total lifelessness
    — nights which refreshed
        the tired body,
        instilling in the quiet limbs
        a wild vigor
        for taking on the new day.
And through all this my parents
were watching,
    caring,
    guarding,
    feeding,
    smiling,
    protecting,
    loving.
And for these I give You thanks —
    for these who have channeled
    so much of Your love, Your chiding,
    Your care, Your forgiveness,

        Your joy into my life;
        for those to whom I've shown
        my gratitude and love so late
        — and so inadequately.
Hear my prayer for them
        and keep them in Your loving care.
And give me grace to be an
        instrument of Yours
        to bring
        that care to them.
And one thing more, O Lord:
        I honor those dear ones
        best when I honor You.
So help me to remember Your
invitation to call You Father,
        that I may prove a worthy child,
        and thankful, too —
eager to do what You want done;
pointing those about me by words and acts
        to You who spreads
        a table for Your family where
        we find forgiveness,
            strength,
            perspective,
            meaning for our lives,
            and joy
            and peace.
Now, Father, all is well.

Amen.

IN ALL OF THESE PEOPLE I FIND YOU

It is a surprise to me, Lord,
How You keep coming to me
through other people.
I have been surprised this way so often.
But I shouldn't be surprised at all,
      because You have promised
      that it would be this way;
      promised that You would live
      in those who loved You;
      and promised that we would find You
      when we brought Your love
      to people who needed it.
Perhaps because there are so many people,
Lord —
      and they so often hurt each other
      and fear each other
      and don't feel comfortable with each other —
perhaps that's why
      I too am somewhat hesitant and careful,
      defensive and suspicious . . .
      especially when I am in strange places
      and with people I know only casually,
      or do not know at all.
You know me, Lord, quite well:
      my edginess,
      my feelings of inadequacy
          that I try so hard
          to conceal.
But You come to me
      like a father,
      smiling,

>   half chiding, but altogether loving
>   as if to say again,
>   "Oh, you of little faith!"
> The infant I lift up,
>   soft, head warm on my cheek,
>   small, a newly baptized one
>   who captures my heart;
> the frightened child
> whom I embrace
>   and who rewards me with his trust;
> the empty, lonely one —
> teen-ager
> or very aged
> for whom I find (or make) time
>   and spend it with him,
> but who enriches me
>   with new perspectives
>   and new dimensions;
> and those who in small groups
>   taste wine and bread
>   with me
>   at Your altar,
> or who listen with me
> to Your Word,
> or who sit and talk and plan
>   together
>   about possibilities
>   for greater and more meaningful
>   service to You and
>   to Your people
>   in this world —
> in all of these
>   I find You
>   speaking with eyes that care,
>   a smile that reassures,
>   hands that welcome
>   expressions of warmth,

        and understanding
        and love and forgiveness
        and acceptance
        and support
        and new opportunities
        and invitation
        to new experiences of oneness
        in You.
The cross,
        symbol of love
        reaching down to me
        in my deepest insecurity,
        and of love embracing me
        with others who are Yours,
becomes a reality.
And I say,
overawed and humbled
and joyously:
        Thank You, Lord!

Amen.

COME INTO THIS NIGHT

There are nights, O Lord,
when Your people,
        childlike,
        totally tired and exhausted,
lie down and fall into instant sleep.
There are nights too when some
would like to sleep but simply cannot
      set aside the thoughts
      that keep them from slumber:
      the excitement of the day just past
         or of tomorrow,
      the worries and the fears
         about uncertainties.
there are nights
for others that are cruelly torn
      by sharp pain,
      bitter grief,
      agonizing loneliness,
      dreams that frighten,
      terrifying interruption.
Come into this night, O Lord,
with Your beauty and Your love
      and power;
      for the darkness cannot
         hide us from You,
      for day and night are both
         alike to You.
Help me to trust You
      and entrust myself to You
         completely this night.
And in the morning be still to me

my constant Companion and my Strength
as I try to live that day — Your day —
for Your purposes:
>wisely,
>courageously,
>lovingly,
>joyfully,

through the power and goodness of Christ.

Amen.

HELP ME TO RUB SLEEP FROM MY EYES

The ability to open my eyes this morning, Lord,
and to take inventory of my surroundings
is a gift.
Some whose eyes have never seen —
or now have ceased to see —
awaken to darkness
        and for vision must depend
        upon rememberings
        and imaginings.
To waken to the sound of birds
        or bells
        or friendly, busy voices
        or music
        or simply noise —
        that is a gift, too.
Some this morning awaken
to the strange and lonely silence
that encloses those who cannot hear,
        who intently read or feel
        the lips of those who would address them,
        who, reaching out to touch,
        long for communication.
I often, Lord, forget these gifts
as I hurry from my bed
and go through the customary readying
that sets me for the day.
And I see little
and am reluctant to hear much,
half resentful at having to leave my bed,
half preoccupied with my anticipating
        the demands of the day.

Let my ears be open
to hear the deep sighs
and bitter sobs hidden behind the masks
that troubled people wear:
> overbusyness,
> and short and curt answers,
> the masks of flippant comments
> and superficial small talk.

Help me to rub sleep from my eyes
that I may see the full range
of possibilities You offer me in this day:
to see the goodnesses
You supply,
so that I am fit to meet
those possibilities;
to love the people who need love;
to encourage those who are wilting
> under pressures;

to call back to purposeful living
those who have given up;
to help give direction
to those who are confused;
to do acts that reflect concern
> for those who have abandoned hope
> because they have found none who care.

And let Your ears be open
to my call for strength.
And let Your eyes be open
to my inabilities,
and Your hand be ever upon me
to lead me
and hold me fast
as I walk in the path,
and in the strength
of Jesus Christ, my Savior.

Amen.

BOOKS, FOOD, PEOPLE BORE ME

I am inclined to believe it, Lord,
    when someone says
    that boredom is akin to hatred.
    When I am bored with books,
        I hate the sight of them.
    And certain foods that I've had
        over and over and over
           again
        I come to resent
        and would rather not eat.
    And some people bore me.
        And I wish they would go away
        and stay away.
    Worst of all, I sometimes get
        bored with myself;
        I know myself so well
        and I become hard
        for myself to like.
I must confess too, Lord: Sometimes
    I am bored with prayers,
    and with some sermons,
    and with the Scriptures,
     and with so much of pious, churchy,
    and religious talk.
    I find myself not listening;
        and I seem to hate it.
    No, I don't hate You, God.
    Or is my boredom really
        my grumbling against You?
Have I failed to see
Your generous hand?

Have I failed to see what is around me
as gifts from You?
And those difficult-to-love people:
Have I failed to see that You have
    sent them to me —
    and me to them —
        to love generously and well?
And when I've become disenchanted
with myself, have I forgotten
that I am a son of Yours, that You
have invested in me trust and power
to convey Your love and profound regard
for people to others?
Forgive me, Lord, mainly for forgetting You,
forgetting Your personal concern for me,
    forgetting the intimate meaning
        of the manger
    and of the cross
    and of the table with the
        bread and the cup.
Help me to understand the love and strength in these
    gifts reserved for me.
    For if I love
        and am loved,
    life takes on a new excitement.
    I am in love —
        Your love.
Now I can be excited about today —
    about where I am,
        what I do,
            whom I'm with —
    about myself,
because I am excited about You.
    And I'm grateful.

Amen.

SUNDAY ROUTINE — OLD FAMILIAR PATTERN

Lord, this day
church buildings
are busy places again.
    Great doors swing on great hinges
    in great cathedrals;
    and dilapitated doors with worn-out knobs
    hang loosely on the tired
    little storefront churches;
    and bells sound out
    in white framed, steepled buildings
    in the countryside.
    But most of them
    have been quiet and museum-like
    for much of the week.
"Come unto me," they say,
but not too many come
if it isn't Sunday.
Today they come:
    some busy, rushing about,
    tending to bulletins and prayer books
    and altar utensils and thermostats
    and chairs and ventilation and flowers,
    and shushing running, noisy children;
    and some to kneel or sit
    in quiet somber dignity;
    some with furrowed brows
    and troubled faces;
    some utterly exhausted
    looking starved for just one moment
    to relax in silence;
    some happy ones

        who can hardly wait to sing
        a boisterous hymn of praise;
        some are there, it seems,
        only in body, and minds are far away —
        a hundred miles or
        a hundred months away.
And I, Lord?
        How am I here?
        It is all so familiar:
        the hymns,
        the prayers,
        the Scripture —
        all such an old, familiar pattern.
Lord, keep this day
        from being mere routine,
        a thing of habit,
        of going through
        the motions and the words.
It is so easy to care less
about this day.
And that is strange
when I am so full of cares:
        cares of this past week,
            of my whole life
            that heap themselves so high,
        cares about myself
        and my tomorrows,
            my debts,
            my unfinished tasks,
            my deadlines,
            my hurdles and obstacles.
Today, this hour, Lord,
I need to be reminded
that You care!
        With the Good Word,
            the Holy Supper,
            the people in whom You live

You care for me.
This day help me
scrape off
the crust of preoccupation with myself,
the scales of forgetfulness,
the shell of boredom.
> Give me that Word of strength
> That I may care for others,
> the uncared for
> and the careless.
> Let me bring to others
> the same loving care
> You bring to me.

I want to use this day
carefully, Lord,
for You
and Yours.

Amen.

EARS, EYES, HANDS, AND LIPS

Why can ears, sensitive to adjust
    fine tuning on high fidelity phonographs—
why can those ears not be sensitive
    to note the pain and despair
    in the voices
    of hurt and weary people?
Why can eyes that have been trained
    to look at a lighted glass tube
    and have seen the craters
    on the moon
    and spaceships orbiting the skies—
why can those eyes not see
    behind the walls of cold little shacks
    and smelly tenements
    to see the crumbled plaster,
        the broken chairs, the empty shelves,
        the poverty and hopelessness?
Why can hands, so deft at playing instruments,
    at guiding the steering wheel,
    at wielding delicate tools,
    at performing a thousand tasks of skill—
why can those hands not reach out
    to help, to lift up, to work with those
        whose hands have grown
            stiff with abuse; or
            limp because they never were allowed
                to take hold on the things
                of life; or
            awkward because they have never
                been shown how?
Why can lips that speak of baseball scores

       and recipes and gardening
       and their children and their jobs
       and the weather and their political concerns
       and even their church —
why can those lips not speak
       lovingly to those who have long been
              unloved and unwanted,
       firmly to those who accept the patterns
              of exclusiveness and snobbery,
       courageously to all men,
              protesting every injustice?
The eyes of Christ have looked
              and seen
              and wept
              and closed in death
       so that our eyes might
       be open to a new and different kind of life —
              His life!
The ears of Christ have heard
       the prayers of the forgotten
       and have been open
              to those of us who will plead for mercy
              in the awareness of our failure
              to love Him and
              His people well.
The lips of Christ speak
       the words that censure those
              who can only love themselves;
              speak the invitation
              to return to waiting arms
              that once hung stretched
                     while He paid with His life.
       Those lips say again the words:
              "Father, forgive them!"
       They speak the empowering words to us:
              "As the Father has sent Me, even so send I you,"
              bestowing love

and full life on other men.
O Lord, who made us and called us into the Body of Christ,
help us to be faithful members of that Body,
to be eyes for God in the world
that seek out people in need,
ears for God
that listen for the sighing
and sobbing of weary and frightened
and frustrated people.
Help us to be hands for God that will hold
and lift and sustain
those who have been rendered
powerless and helpless
by the circumstances of life and
the thoughtlessness of men.
Help us to be lips for God that plead
the cause of the hopeless,
that speak welcome, friendship,
to those who have been made
to feel so very alone,
that men may see You
and have life
and have strength
and have joy.

Amen.

I AM PART OF THE RUSHING AND CHANGING

Everything goes so fast, Lord:
    the turning of calendar leaves,
    the cars and trains and planes,
    birthdays,
    the way children grow tall,
    the ticking of watches,
    the chiming of clocks;
    and wrinkles
    and dimming of vision
    and graying and thinning of hair.
And there are more changes, Lord:
    old buildings vacated
        and getting older,
    and some torn down,
    and new ones — shining, modern, and glassy;
    and miles and miles
    of concrete covered with speeding —
        and sometimes crawling —
    lines of cars
    pressing in opposite directions.
    And I need to remember
    in the rushing and the changing:
    I am here, rushing too
        and changing,
but never quite rushing away from myself.
And, however I might change,
I am very much myself —
    the self I know so well —
with all my all-too-human ways:
    my prideful ways,
    my defensiveness,

        my jealousies,
        my suspicions,
        my self-seeking and false modesty,
        my shortsightedness and impatience,
        my self-pity and self-indulgence,
and my little faith.
I hate all this;
        I wish that I could rush from them
            and change myself.
But You have neither hurried from me
nor changed Your ways toward me,
and Your presence and Your ways
        are love
        and compassion
        and forgiveness
        and strength for new possibilities.
And that is reason enough to be glad.
Help me to slow down
        and see the gifts You have given me:
            Your words,
            Your love,
            Your people
            and the love they give,
            and with it the opportunity
            to love You through loving them.
And help me to be stable
        and unchanging,
        dependable and steadfast,
            reliable and consistent in my loving,
that those around me,
plagued by speed and frightened by change,
may find Your constant concern for them in me.
        But make me hurry, Lord,
        to find ways to use my fleeting days well.
        And make me flexible,
        willing and able
        to change myself and my ways

to be
> open-eared — to hear the cries
> for help all around;
> open-eyed — to see those who need
> part of what You've given
> to me in abundance;
> open-armed — to welcome those who need
> companionship
> and are lonely;
> open-handed — to share with those
> who have little or nothing
> that of which I have more
> than I need;
> open-hearted — to receive and to give
> the love that You implant
> deep within men.

And one thing more, Lord:
> Keep this prayer from being mere words —
> and let me speak and act,
>> remembering the Christ who loved
>> children who had been pushed aside,
>> and women who had been abused,
>> and men whose spirits had been broken,
>> and me.

Amen.

YOU THOUGHT OF ME LONG AGO

God, I find it hard
        to believe that
        You remember
        me.
There are so many who call You
        "Father"
        and expect You to help them
                in some special need,
            to accompany them
                in their travels,
            to attend them in
                their loneliness,
            to stand with them
                in a difficult
                or dangerous
                encounter:
            surgeons, pilots,
            homesick children,
            prisoners, cab drivers,
            nurses, policemen,
            farmers, construction
            workers on tall buildings,
            coal miners, railroad switchmen,
            motel maids, hospital orderlies,
            mail carriers, bedfast grandmothers
            and old men in wheelchairs and men
            who drive huge earth-moving equipment
            and thousands more. . . .
And You have promised to hear their prayers.
        You keep count
        on all the birds,

    and control and direct the rains
    and clouds and winds,
    and cause the seeds
    to sprout, and fruit
    to develop full and sweet.
And I believe it.
But I find it
hard to remember You.
Even in my prayers,
for which I set aside
brief times so that nothing else
    might interrupt
    and I might concentrate alone
    on You —
even there I find myself
so often only saying words —
coming with
    "Lord, Lord" on my lips,
    with heart and thoughts
    devoted to a hundred
    other objects
      of my affections
      or of my worries.
And when my prayer is ended,
I wonder what I've said!
I say: "Lord, think on me!"
but I promptly turn away
to live as if You were not near
    or were not even real.
And often enough when
    tempted to selfishness,
      to grumbling and pouting
      to meanness and short temper,
      to dishonesty and
        phoniness,
I do not even think that
You have thoughts about what

confronts me then.
Help me, O God,
to know You thought of me
long, long ago —
long before I ever thought of You;
that I have been
the object of Your concern
and tender love;
that Bethlehem was
        planned for me,
    and the hill
        with three crosses,
    and the place
        where the stone
        was rolled
        away.
Help me remember
    that my coming
    to faith
    was not my idea
        but Yours —
            Your goodness.
Then remembering
how well I've been remembered
by You,
I — by Your love — may be enabled
to remember to serve
You well
and love You well this day;
    in the power of Christ
        and Your Holy Spirit.

Amen.

BREAK THE QUIET WITH YOUR LOVE

I sit in quiet darkness . . .
    no noisy bands here,
    no screaming crowds
    or roaring engines;
    no dazzling neon,
    no glaring floodlights . . .
        quiet darkness!
Darkness reminiscent of
    the hours before You called
    upon the earth's first light to shine;
    or the first night
    the first man spent away from Eden,
    frightened;
    or the forty terror-filled days
    of living in the belly of the ark while
    rains drove fiercely against her timbers;
    or the night of our Lord
    in Gethsemane — that night of anguished prayer
    and betrayal;
    or the dark night in the locked room
    where after their Master's death
    the eleven fear-filled disciples hid;
    the kind of night that prompted
    one man to make the plaintive cry:
        "I wait for the Lord,
        more than they that watch
        for the morning!"
Still my anxieties, Lord!
Place Your sure hand on me.
Speak the word of forgiveness
    and peace.

Break the quiet with Your love.
Through the darkness
        of this night,
Jesus, You will be my light.
Listen to me, hear me pray.
Wake me to a blessed day.

Amen.